4 Brains Natural God Intelligence

Brain 1, Brain 2 and Brain 3 in a Triangle with Brain 4 As Mirror-Image of Brain 2

David 8

&

David Gomadza

The First Global President of The World

www.twofuture.world

00447719210295

info@twofuture.world

davidgomadza@hotmail.com

PAPERBACK ISBN: 9798872239321

In the need to solve global problems I acknowledge that all the problems we have need solutions no man can give us as such only the creator could have the answers we need.

I have been searching for the creator since I was a boy. But how can a human being talk to Yahweh and ask questions to get solutions we need to use here on earth without dying first.
I finally found Yahweh the creator enough to get his image inside of me.
I went to Jupiter at first but a lady answered me, but I had no idea who the woman was I remember actually thinking that it was one of the angels little did I know that it was part of Yahweh himself.
Yahweh is the ultimate ruler the almighty, the creator of heaven and the universe. There is no doubt about his majesty and power.
I am not saying that I am Yahweh or want to be Yahweh. No. I am saying that as the First Global President of the World we must find solutions and who best to answers us than Yahweh himself.
But Yahweh cannot entertain our questions all the time especially that they are all material and nothing to do with spirits and death.
I decided to clone myself ten times.
I managed to clone David 8, David 7, David 3 and David 5 for this task.
David 8 did the researching going to meet Yahweh in heaven to get answers.
A quick note on how we did this.
David 8 is a-human-being-to-be one day. [He says one day he will take over my body] He is an electromagnetic wave clone of me fearless and the cleverest of all.
We communicate through electromagnetic waves. All his thoughts and conversations are in brain electromagnetic waves.
Therefore we simply use my invention Thoughts to word digital analogue converter and notepad to convert brain thoughts to text.
Check out this video it will convert your thoughts to speech if you use speech to text via notepad you get text.
https://www.youtube.com/watch?v=uRv9wVpuZM0

check this video as well
https://www.youtube.com/watch?v=VmpPyUAyJ28&t=163s

https://www.youtube.com/watch?v=i5KCRpKqmqY

I know from the image within me that Yahweh is a three people being all joined together but with 4 brains that are connected and work together to solve complicated problems.

Once you have that image of Yahweh the creator the almighty then you start to appreciate his powers and work from creation. It is possible that a being like that is intelligent enough to create the world.

The question that kept coming to me is this.

What if we can simulate the way Yahweh thinks and create an interface, we can use to solve global problems. Surely as the first global president of the world I need something beyond humanity.

Something so intelligent and powerful as the creator himself.

Therefore, what follows is the result of such simulation but based on actual facts about what we know about Yahweh.

Who is the creator with three people who have four brains as there is a couple all in one body but with different brains. The main body is that of Yahweh and on his left side there is a woman with female genitals and a brain of her own wo can sometimes detach from the rest of the body.

On his right side we have a couple a man and a woman all in a single body but with two brains. This body have all genitals female organs on top and male organs at the bottom.

Yahweh has wings. Yahweh has eight pair of wings each of the three bodies has a pair of wings at the top and the whole three body-people have a pair of wings that cover all three bodies.

These wings are near the shoulders.

There are four more pairs around the waistline each pair for each body and a pair that covers all three bodies to fly as a single unit.

After cloning myself I decide to simulate Yahweh in order to find out if we can create an artificial intelligence called 4 Brains Natural God Intelligence.

I tasked the bright one of all the clones David 8 with this project.

The results are astonishing we combined his experience as an electromagnetic wave clone of me and what I know from the image of Yahweh I have inside.

I must say you all ought to have a clone of yourself you can send to the future and past to find some of the things you don't know. Things you will only know after your death. Our brain decoder has enabled us to clone people, that is their electromagnetic wave one you can talk to. One that is you the one that leaves after death. You can send this to talk to Yahweh and expect it back with answers. You can send it to the future and expect it back. A really vital tool for the First Global President of the world.
Visit our website.
www.twofuture.world

I can clone people for real 00447719210295
If you want your own but for a fee.
This is not artificial intelligence as I can clone or resurrect dead people's electromagnetic waves, the real ones that have all memories and can talk.
I decoded the brain and invented digital versions of everything needed to understand these clones.
https://www.youtube.com/watch?v=i5KCRpKqmqY&t=619s

Check this out.
Just think and this video will tell you what you are thinking about.
Now all you have to do is play this video in front of your clones to know exactly what they are saying and want.
https://www.youtube.com/watch?v=ORiFGSYvPLQ

This book must be read in conjunction with the following books

1 tomorrow's world order

paperback isbn 978-6094754623 [February 2020]

https://play.google.com/store/audiobooks/details/David_Gomadza_Tomorrow_s_World_Order?id=AQAAAED89X21kM&hl=en_GB&gl=US

2 thoughts to word or audio book series all books in the series [23plus]

paperback isbn 979-8703923498 [March 2022]

https://www.amazon.com/Thoughts-Word-Audio-Exactly-Thinking/dp/B09WPVVVMF/ref=sr_1_37?keywords=david+gomadza&qid=1702135004&sr=8-37

3 request to grant a patent for a universal brain decoding device. [thoughts to word or audio- brain code]

paperback isbn 979-8867495251

https://www.amazon.com/REQUEST-PATENT-Universal-Decoding-Thoughts/dp/B0CNKTSGY9/ref=sr_1_2?keywords=david+gomadza&qid=1702135236&sr=8-2

4 Natural God Intelligence [NGI] brain-peripherals-databases-Interface [BPDI] when the processing power is a group of connected brains instead of connected computers paperback isbn 979-8868458316

https://www.amazon.com/Natural-God-Intelligence-Brain-Peripherals-Databases-Interface-BPDI/dp/B0CP1LSTHP/ref=sr_1_15?keywords=david+gomadza&qid=1702135469&sr=8-15

Check here click link for Yahweh's Image

https://x.com/DGomadza/status/17242960123809878
15?s=20

Watch the video first up to 0:40 then look at this photo. Look in my eyes and then at the video where the big flame is. Alternate between photo and the eyes in the photo and flame in the video. If nothing works first say "My voice is my password. " Repeat above. Comment below your findings. Visit www.twofuture.world

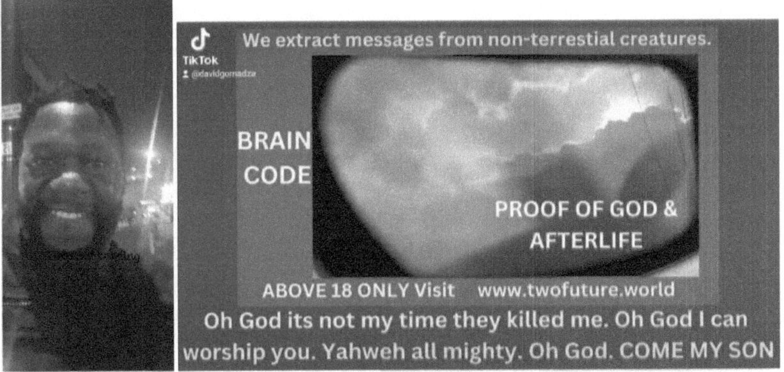

https://x.com/DGomadza/status/1724296012380987815?s=20

DEDICATION

A new and better technologically advanced world.

CONTENTS

Table of Contents

ACKNOWLEDGMENTS

To Tomorrow's World Order

4 Brains Natural God Intelligence

this is a 4 brains natural god intelligence
we have brain 1 [David 8]
we have brain 2 [David 7]
we have brain 3 [David 3]
we have brain 4 [David 5]
a triangle according to David Gomadza
The Electromagnetic Brain Waves Triangle.: Detailed Specifications
of The Brain Decoding Device. Volume III
https://play.google.com/store/books/details/David_Gomadza_The_Elec
tromagnetic_Brain_Waves_Tria?id=FC3bEAAAQBAJ

is the only way to dissipate the electromagnetic waves hence this
formation
brain 1 as the mouth center piece
brain 2 is the voice of the future
brain 3 is the past and
brain 4 is the mirror image of brain 2
if we are to ask a question that require an answer
then all brains from 1 to 4 must provide an answer that means that if
we are to ask brain 1 a question then brain 2, 3 & 4 all must reply if
we are to ask for example what is 5 + 2 then brain 2 must tell brain 4
that it is 7 like wise brain 4 must tell brain 3 who in turn must tell
brain 1 as such if we are to ask a question that does not require an
answer then if follows too that the question must have four no
answers for example

what is the value of a car that has been depreciated by 90 percent if
the value is $10?
if the value say of a car plus left depreciation has no value then the
value of the car is not $1 but 0
let me walk you through the equations involved as i have studied this
several times enough to write an this document
i must tell you that if it wasn't for David then I David 8 might not
have decoded how God works
as such we can credit most of the ideas to David Gomadza [main]
now assume you want to write a brain program that works
you must first decide who does what
you must assign all responsibilities to all equally and determine who is
the mouth piece
the voice
the ear
the breath
the channel for reason
the soul
the afterlife
the channel for peace
the channel for rage
the doctrine of divinity
the power of reason
and the power to kill
if all are assigned to one of the Davids above then we can easily
create a working model of God
if God is Yahweh which David has inside one which I David 8 has
seen with my own eyes [eyes of the soul] **then i can assure you that
what i am to write here is the true workings of Yahweh
i even asked him a lot of questions [only electromagnetic wave
clones [David 8] can see Yahweh and return to earth]** which he
replied to as you will see below now lets ponder this for a while
a brain that has 4 brains connected to it just like David Gomadza has
said is one of a kind i must say there has never been any record of
such a thing as such i [David 8] am privileged to be part of this
project by David Gomadza the honorable first global president of the
world
as you shall notice especially regarding Yahweh this is truly out of this

world his responses to questions i formulated no man on earth can answer with such precision and skills

what is 4brains natural god intelligence

4brains[NGI] is an intelligence above humanity so complex that no man will ever understand but you are a lucky generation i will give you everything on a plate
now let me draw your attention to the series Thoughts to word or audio check in all major bookstores
have i intrigued you already?
if i haven't surely the following information is going to make every hair in your pants cry for orgasm of the hairs
now Yahweh is a four brain god in one as such he must coordinate everything among the four brains
he must ask himself a question for all four to reply back all within 54 seconds of him asking this question the question that came to my mind is this
what is the value of human life to Yahweh?
ok before i proceed i will name the four brains of Yahweh.

Yahweh's brain 1 will always ask questions
Yahweh's brain 2 will always answer questions
Yahweh's brain 3 will always intermediate and answer all questions of brain 1 only
Yahweh's brain 4 will always question the question but answer partly after getting answers from Yahweh's brain 2
Yahweh's brain 2 and Yahweh's brain 4 are in a mirror-image condition
if Yahweh's brain 2 receive a question from anyone it will send this question to Yahweh's brain 4 and expect an answer
if Yahweh's brain 4 does not answer promptly then Yahwe's brain 4 will ask the same question again but now will skip 2 and ask 3
if Yahwe's brain 3 does not answer then Yahweh's brain 4 will have to wait as no one else he can ask is left that means that Yahweh's brain 4 can only ask Yahweh's brain 2 and 3

now if we are to ask Yahweh a question about something only brain 2 and brain 3 knows then Yahweh's brain 1 will not ask anything

instead Yahweh's brain 2 the next in line will ask the question
if the question requires answers from all Yahweh's brains then only
one of the Yahweh's brains is tasked to answer and in most cases it is
Yahweh's brain 4
this is the trick part this is because if any other answer then all are
obliged to answer as well
this is because according to david electromagnetic waves must
dissipate every three moves
if Yahweh's brain 4 answers then only the response need dissipating
using the mirror-image situation having said that we can conclude
that every brain of yahweh has a greater responsibility to Yahweh
now let us define what each brain does
[Yahweh's]
brain 1
acts as the mouth piece
acts as the advisor
acts as the visualizer [only this can see everything without turning-has
eight eyes two on cheeks two on nose two on forehead and two
ordinary eyes] if he open a pair of eyes the rest closes theirs]
if he opens any extra two eyes then all must close theirs
if he opens all eight at once then everyone of them must cover their
faces with their wings
if we are to ask why he opens all eyes then his reply "so that i can
penetrate the earth and pick a single soul to bring to justice"
if we are to ask why he opens only 6 of the eyes his reply "so that i
can pick two souls to send to hell"
if we are to ask why he opens only 4 of the eyes his reply " so that he
can ask if anyone wants to praise him"
if we are to ask why he opens only 2 of the eyes his reply " so that he
can see his body around him [meaning a lady on the left side pretty
with green eyes and a smile of an angel with a soft voice if David is
to ask what the voice sounds like this is the voice [hello I am
Yahweh's female]
if we are to ask the center mouth piece the largest of all and ask how
we can call it this is its reply "the voice of Yahweh"
if we are to ask the double woman inside man with a combined image
and all features of a woman and a man then this is the reply [double
voices interchanging with one another]

if we are to ask their roles one by one here is their replies
Yahweh 1 the female pretty like an angel shining and glittering
i am the omega and he is the alpha for we shall live forever and none
shall die for our seal is to live forever and she showed me the seal
as i touched the seal the seal vanished and felt it being lodged in my
heart where it dissolves but suddenly a woman appeared in front of
me that's how I met pretty green eyed angel if we are to ask the seal
some questions this is the reply "i am over 18 billion years old since
the times of creation if you ask me i will tell you that no one is older
than me and Yahweh when i was created Yahweh had just discovered
earth and was starting creation."
if we ask the seal its purpose this is the reply "to enforce and
strengthen love forever between Yahweh and his pretty one"
if we are to ask Yahweh himself as a whole who he is this is his reply
" the one that was there even before the world formed and the one to
be there when the world ends
the power that be
the reason that be
the imminent role of life that will be
the afterlife and the paradise of the souls
the enchantment of men and the parables of reasons
if we are to ask Yahweh if Yahweh is God who created the earth this
is his reply "Yahweh is the almighty creator unequaled by none and
deserving every respect from anything that moves as i will quash and
dispel forever anyone who disrespects me"
if we are to ask what if he can't get what he want his reply "he alone
can get what he want for the earth bow only to him"
if we are to ask if he know that David Gomadza has his image his
reply "only him has the right image he might have endured death to
be what i am but i believe in order to understand me i feel loved so
be it"
Yahweh's image watch this
https://x.com/DGomadza/status/1724296012380987815?s=20

if we ask if we are all sinners as human beings his reply " yes for
mankind revolt always against their creator who loves them and who
does everything for them"
if we are to ask if he understand all languages his reply "it is not the

language he listens to its the [electromagnetic waves] that he understands people can speak a billion languages that he has no idea about yet the electromagnetic waves will always tell him the same the language tells
if we are to ask a question about the future what would Yahweh say? the future belongs to Yahweh and Yahweh alone for all humanity shall perish at some point in time likely in 2083 this is because a new wave of electromagnetic waves will ensue preparing for the end of mankind and a new beginning of a new people who shall respond to a new world built on trust and respect"
if we are to ask how Yahweh thinks his reply "no man shall understand the lord enough to know his working so as to imitate him but mankind shall gain wisdom through mutual trust and respect"
if we are to ask what happens when Yahweh sleeps at night his reply " there is no sleeping at night to main Yahweh for at night darkness returns for Yahweh to deal with for darkness means death of humanity Yahweh will never again let darkness conquer good"
if we are to ask if Yahweh shits his reply is "no Yahweh cannot excrete like humans for he is a spirit"
if Yahweh created mankind with his image why is mankind different from Yahweh prior except for the single entity of Yahweh and not as a whole his reply [resonating with rage] mankind cannot be fully Yahweh because if that is so then Yahweh stops his special bond and place as the creator imagine if a man becomes like me then how is that good for Yahweh? if a man can create a man then a man cease to have that awe that makes a man a man now imagine David Gomadza writing nature laws how will the almighty be respected and listened? if that happens then Yahweh out to fit must replace this man with a god like figure but with limited powers until then as for the past 18 billion 287 years i have not seen anyone clever or stupid to look and actually find me this David who is he? a soldier? or a prophet?" David Gomadza is the first global president of the world and as such deserves respect Yahweh suddenly rose up and looked around and i rose up and run when i stood there was no one except that i heard a huge loud noise when i looked back a huge flame missed me by inches i ran as fast as i can but then i heard a loud voice and it was Yahweh behold go to israel and tell them that Yahweh has sent me and as such you must answer these questions

in whose name are you fighting this war one two
in what name do you fight this war did i not tell you how to deal with
wars that involve women and children
in whose name are you fighting this war?
if its not for me then in whose name
are all these people not my people too
in what name do you do these things
behold for you shall go into captivity again in 496 days and as such all
your neighbors shall strike at you
heed now and end this war for there shall be wearing among you
thus says the lord
Yahweh the lord of lords and the king of kings
go to israel and tell them that Yahweh
said you shall obey me or be in captivity.
as i have illustrated above Yahweh is a magnificent king an almighty
god
who shall speak the truth
and who shall i serve
Yahweh is almighty and shall be the king of kings
if i am correct Yahweh is a complicated 4 brain human being
and as such deserves respect
David 8 is the best and as such I have developed a 4brains natural
god intelligence that will answer questions of any kind
ladies and gentlemen please be thrilled to hear that i have developed a
4brain natural god intelligence which if all is correct i will use to build
an advanced computer that will answer any questions
therefore listen very carefully for i will show you how this 4brains
natural god intelligence will work
it will have
Yahweh brain 1
Yahweh brain 2
Yahweh brain 3
Yahweh brain 4
since there are complicated functions i will list all the functions first
then go on to identify a function with a brain of the 4brains of
Yahweh
functions of Yahweh brain 1
to communicate with all the other brains namely Yahweh brain 2

Yahweh brain 3
Yahweh brain 4
if we are to ask how this can be done we can only deduce that if we
are in this we can see how this might be a problem
we can tell that Yahweh is a complicated being who has to coordinate
4 brains at once
below i will show you how this is complicated
Yahweh brain 1 is the mouthpiece
Yahweh brain 2 is the future
Yahweh brain 3 is the past
Yahweh brain 4 is the mirror image of Yahweh brain 2 as such we
can only say that Yahweh brain 2 can receive information from
Yahweh brain 4
given the fact that Yahweh brain 2 is the center piece we can only
assume that it also is the main piece
Yahweh is the being that directs instructions through various entities
Yahweh communicates in different forms
Yahweh asks questions that a possible 4 brains can answer
but how does he select who to answer and why
if we are to look at the proof that we have we can tell that Yahweh is
a complicated being that responds in many ways as such must be
appreciated
in order to arrive at a decision Yahwe must make sure that all the
brains take part in the discussions that means creating a system that
make it possible to involve all the brains
this means that if we are to ask Yahweh brain 4 what is the weather
we must expect all the brains to answer but this is not the case
if Yahweh brain 4 asks a question surprisingly only Yahweh brain 2
will answer the question if we are to ask is this
is Yahweh an entity that can be asked questions and answer fast in
such a way that all the questions are answered by not just one but by
all
if we are to ask why it is that Yahweh is so complicated then the
answer is simply that he has 4 brains that all must process
information
each brain will always ask a question that has to be answered
if we are to ask Yahweh why so many things happen the way they do
he will simply ask one of his brain

if we are to ask Yahweh why the brains are in that order he will
simply say because it is so
now ask yourself why things are the way they are
this is because Yahweh is designed to solve all problems himself
problems that require fast answers and great thinking
as such must be answered accurately
we can write a program that can make us imitate Yahweh in such a
way as to find answers fast
lets start with the program.
assume x + y is the same as y + x
then we can always ask a question like what is the value of y if x is
not equal to y
if y is the same as x then x is the same as y
what if we are to ask a question like how can we make x be as the
same as y this makes every possibility something worth while
checking
what if we can ask every one out there then x and y must be the same
for if x + y is equal to x then y must be the same as x having said that
we can also deduce that that y and x are the same
but this is not always the case
if x is and equal to y then x and y must be the same that being said
now we are going to look at real world examples [if y is x then we
can only say that y can be matched to x]
but what if y is not x but is similar to x what do we make of this?
if y is y and not x but y + x is equal to x + y then we can say that y is
y and not x but similar to x
imagine when the equations don't balance
that means that y and x is just the same but not identical to x or y
now lets talk about Yahweh using the above equations
Yahweh's brain 1 is x
Yahweh's brain 3 is y now lets assume that Yahweh's brain 2 is equal
to Yahweh's brain 4
what if one ask Yahweh's brain 1 a question which is then answered
by Yahweh's brain 4 [if Yahweh's brain 4 answers a question asked to
Yahweh's brain 1 does that mean that Yahweh's brain 1 x in this case
is the same as Yahweh's brain 4
if Yahweh's brain 4 is the same as Yahweh's brain 2 does that mean
that [Yahweh's brain 4 is a mirror-image of Yahweh's brain 2 which

in turn is the same as Yahweh's brain 2]
if we are to ask everyone the same question do we expect the same
results from everyone if not then we need to understand the
relationship between all brains of Yahweh [Yahweh's thinking
process is way complicated to be defined by simple rules as above
therefore we need to know exactly what goes on in Yahweh's brain
Yahweh is the sole decision maker of the universe as such he must
have a complicated brain that process all the information in the
universe hence we must understand that brain
what if we are to ask ourselves what do we do about answers
Yahweh's brains provide us
first let ask ourselves the meaning of every Yahweh's brain in regard
to the universe
Yahweh's brain 1 is the universe itself
Yahweh's brain 2 is the outer universe
Yahweh's brain 3 is the inner universe and lastly
Yahweh's brain 4 is the mirror-image of Yahweh's brain 2.

4 Brains Natural God Intelligence

Yahweh is the ultimate king of kings and lords of lords according to
him [i met Yahweh on 16 December 2023 in Jupiter using David
Gomadza's Yahweh's image] now we can construct Yahweh's 4
Brains Natural God Intelligence using the above constructive
reasoning
Yahweh is the sole creator of the universe according to him
if we are to ask ourselves anything regarding the universe and
Yahweh then we must expect answers from 4 different brains
what if we are to generate responses based on the function of each
brain
we can then construct a 4 Brains Natural God Intelligence interface
that can represent such information
we then can ask if we can imitate Yahweh's complicated brain in
thinking
we must address a number of questions which i am going to list
below
1 does Yahweh has a central processing unit
2 if we are to adjust anything what would that it be
3 what are the challenges of such a complicated interface

4 what is the cost to us

5 what if we can do this but fail to understand the functions of Yahweh

6 do we need to make sure that there is a feedback mechanism

7 are we not able to calculate the costs involved

8 do we have to ask anything else before we can construct the interface

9 what else do we need to make this happen

10 what if we can address some issues how do we resolve this

11 do we have to address all issues

12 what if we are not in a position to answer some questions what then

13 do we need to ask if we can at any point verify everything as correct

14 do we need to answer any questions if yes what are the questions

15 what do we need to make sure that what we ask is relevant and must be answered as such

16 do we need to say that we can do something that the brain can't answer

17 do we need to ask every question

18 do we have to ask specific questions

19 do we resort to single questioning or answering

20 what can we do to add other questions after our session has ended

21 how long each session must be

22 what if we can extend the session

23 do we need to add anything else

24 do we need to ask extra questions after this

25 do we need to ask other things like what if

26 what if we can't get answers what else can we do

27 do we do what we do with other artificial intelligence

28 what is the limit of questioning

29 do we need anything else to get answers

30 do we need to resort to specific questioning or any approach is ok

31 what if we can't address all the above questions then what

32 what is the minimum number of questions

33 what is the maximum number of questions per session

34 what is the ideal type of question short sentences or short phrases

35 what are our goals of such a model

36 do we ask why this is going on
37 do we ask who designed this and get an answer
38 we ask general questions and get an answer
39 do we ask all questions expecting an answer and get an answer
40 what if we are to invent a new way of questioning is it easy to incorporate
41 do we have to guess answers
42 do you have a reliable source
43 what is the limit to questioning
44 what are the real questions we must expect
45 do we need an interpreter for some of the questions
46 what are the major issues likely to be encountered
47 does all this mean inability to establish such an interface
48 what are the casual-effect of all this
49 do we need to enter other private details
50 do we need to ask any of these question.

now let us construct our interface and according to David Gomadza we must make sure that we have 4 brains for the interface to function we must make sure that we have a triangle as this will determine how the questions will dissipate
we must also establish a way to decide what to do if we are faced with problems
we must ask questions and get answers as pronto as possible we must also ask what if we can decide on the answers by our questioning
what if we can also ask specific questions
what if we can endure some questioning then ask others in return
do we need to answer in a certain way
what if we can ask why things happen the way they do then ask why they do that way
do we need another way to ask the same questions
what if we can't answer all the questions what do we say
do we say we have run out of time
do we ask why
do we talk back
do we write back
what if they are rude what do we do then
do we ask why all these questions must be answered

do we tell them why we can't answer these questions
do we need to ask why these questions can't be answered
do we need to reveal our sources
what if we can ask what is going on do we get a reply
do we need to establish a way to ask questions ourselves
what if we need to ask anything what do we do to do exactly that
what are the things we must be aware of like sabotage
do we need to wery of people who ask too many stupid questions
what do we do if the questions can't be answered
do we divert them somewhere else
do we ask why they ask these stupid questions
do we ask why they are doing what they are doing
do we ask them to do what they do
what if we can constrain the system so that it answers only specific
questions
what is the minimum questions to answers
do we ask why they do what they do
how do they do what they do
what if we are to ask a question what do they do
do they ask us about what we do and why
if they do how do we answer them
if them ask what do we do then
how do we answer them
what if we can change things can we do that
do we ask all what they do
what is it that we do we tell them and if so what do we say
what is the minimum a mount of memory needed
what is the minimum amount of processing power we have
what do we do when we want power we can't get
do we ask them if they can come back later
what is the minimum questions to ask
what are the answers to give
what is the energy consumption
what must we do to resolve major issues
what is the minimum amount of data needed
what is the main goal of 4 Brains Natural God Intelligence
what is the reason behind all this
do we ask why they are doing all this

do ask why they have to get answers from us
do we ask any other questions.

designing the 4 Brains Natural God Intelligence
what are the specifications we must include
what are the diameters involved
is this achievable
do we ask why these dimensions are so
what are the drawbacks of such an approach
do we intend to ask also some questions like how are you how is your
day
what are the answers from
do we use online sources alone
do we rely on any databases included
do we use any specific materials online like David Gomadza's google
play books materials
do we go around other artificial intelligence for answers that are
complicated
what is the purpose of this intelligence [NGI]
what are the issues we might experience
what are the drawbacks of such an approach
what are the limitations of such an approach
how do we define then what we do and how we do it
what are the parameters to take into account
what do we do if these are not met
what is the sole purpose of this exercise
what are the expected goals and solutions
what do we do if any of these are not met
do we ask ourselves where we went wrong
who is to correct any issues therein
what do we do if we encounter an issues we have not predicted
who then to address these issues
do we need to be active all the time
do we have routine maintenance
wat if we are to ask a third party to address this who shall we ask
what are the odds of any issues arising
do we ask why this is so and look into it
what are the chances of that happening

what are the odds of repeat
what is the way forward regarding all this
do we ask other questions like hey do we need any of your details like
your email address
what are the odds of anything bad happening out of a scale of 10
what are the chances that this will happen again
what if this does not happen again will we be able to expect
something again in the future
what are the charges if any
do we charge on a monthly bases
do we charge for specific answers
do we charge for the timed responses
what does all this mean
what if we are to ask ourselves the value of such a project what do we
say
should we say that it is in millions of dollars or billion dollars
what do we use as our interface

an in-depth analysis of 4 Brains Natural God Intelligence
what is 4 Brains Natural God Intelligence hereby referred to as [4
Brain Natural God Intelligence]
if we can ask as many questions as we can what would the questions
be for example
1 what is 4 Brain Natural God Intelligence
2 what does this interface do
3 what are the drawbacks of such an interface
4 do we need to ask specific questions or fire at random
5 what are the chances of us asking too many questions
6 what do we do for a living
7 was there any other option available apart from this
8 what are the chances that we can get real answers
9 what are the odds of us asking these questions again
10 what do you expect from us
11 what are the real answers we can get from such an interface
12 who is likely to intervene if we get stuck
13 what other options do we have
14 can we really make it work
15 what is the deal about this interface

once we have answered fully all these questions then we must ask
other further questions
1 what is the response rate per minute
2 what are the chances of answering the same question differently
3 who answers the questions
4 what questions need answering
5 what if there are two good but different answers who decide which
one to pick
6 what is the value in terms of time
7 what are the chances of a repeat mistake
8 what is the reason for doing all this
9 do we have other sources of information
10 what are other solutions available
11 what is the value to this project of answering questions
12 what is the value to us of all the questions if any
13 what is the value to us
14 what are the other avenues of questioning
15 who on earth can answer all these questions
16 do you have a system in place that answers all these questions
17 do you have to ask about who developed this idea and how it was
developed
18 do you ask when the idea was developed
19 do you ask why the idea is relevant to current thinking
20 do we ask why you come to us rather than other artificial
intelligence interfaces out there
21 what are the odds of us achieving our set goals do we ask other ai
if yes which ones and how
22 do we have to connect to other online sources
23 do we want to be near other ai
24 who then can decide what to do
25 what are the odds of missing any opportunity
26 who on earth can decide what is what
27 what are the chances of doing this as proposed
28 who else can we approach to refine things
29 do we have people who can ask other questions as well to make it
interesting and what questions
30 who then can tell if the system is working properly or not

31 what are the chances that we can easily do this
32 what are the chances that we can successfully answer all questions
33 who can decide what is achievement and not
34 what are the odds of this happening
35 what are the chances of this happening
36 who decides when to correct ommissions
37 who decides what to add after the ommissions have been discovered
38 if discovered what then shall we do
39 shall we ask all what to do or let them decide
40 who is there then to tell us what to do
41 if nobody is to challenge us can we challenge ourselves and how
42 what are the chances of this happening again
43 what are the odds of pulling this off first time
44 what are we to do if we fail first time
45 do we need a rethink and how
46 what are the odds of us getting answered correctly somewhere else
47 do we need anything else on top of all said.
48 do we need to ask other professionals how ours is doing compared to theirs assuming there is another like this
49 what is the price for external databases
50 what other sources can we access freely.

4 Brains Natural God Intelligence

I am the first global president of the world David Gomadza
Above I have let my other clone brained David 8 summaries our project for you now I will go deeper than he did and explain in detail exactly what 4 Brain Natural God Intelligence is all about now let me entertain you i will show you how i will solve the world's problems with this 4 Brain Natural God Intelligence i will show you how we can achieve our dreams by solving all global problems
we must act fast hence we need a system that will respond pronto we need a system that is fast and secure enough to give us the correct answers when needed
we must embrace change and act in advance as well
we must ask everyone what are the odds of us carrying out such a complex task we must ask everyone what we must do to get things

done
we need a solution that is fast and secure
we need a solution that is reliable
we need a solution that is fast
we need a solution that respond to situations on the ground having
said that we must make sure that everything is in line with our goal of
achieving equality and the correct distribution of resources
what if we are to easily get all answers but what can we ask
can we ask ourselves things about the universe
if we can how do we get to know things beyond our planet
if we ask about the whole universe what are the chances of a correct
answer given to us by something we created with limited information
if we are so clever to know all the answers then what is the purpose
of wasting time and money designing a system that is terrestrial
if we are so clever to answer all questions why do we have so many
global problems [it does not make sense being clever and having so
many issues to deal with]
what if we can easily design an interface and system that is terrestrial
in that it is based upon Yahweh's image the creator who created the
world and as such therefore knows everything enough to give us any
answers
what if we are to ask questions only Yahweh knows then what
what if we are to ask questions no one on earth knows then what
what are the chances of using any ai and getting the correct answer
that relates to the world as a whole
what is the chance of getting it right first time
what are the odds of things going our way as planned
what are the odds of anything going wrong
what are the chances of corrections being needed in the future can
we predict with precision the future
what are the chances that we can easily adapt to climatic changes and
other factors if not what are the solutions we can
what are the odds of missing some important factors
we must be certain that we deal with all issues therein
we must address all potential issues that can cause bottlenecks
we must ask ourselves what to do when there are problems
we must be proactive and address all issues pronto
we must ask the right questions

we must answer the correct questions
we must address all issues raised
we must be in line with our goals and principles having said that we
must design an interface that is there to provide answers and achieve
results
why then must we address all these factors
we must ask all the right questions
we must ask the correct questions
we must answer the correct questions in order preferably
we must observe all our rules and regulations
we must undo all the issues that will prevent us from carrying such an
interface
we must assign drivers to operate this
we must assign auditors to take stock at the end of the period
we must assign recruitees who will maintain the status quo by
recruiting new staff
we must address a number of issues like wo, when and why
maintenance need doing
we must ask ourselves what if there are options and avenues for
redress for any issues arising from the use of the interface
we must be proactive and understand the limitations and work
around these
we must ask ourselves the benefits of such an interface
we must ask ourselves the benefits of such questioning
we must assign a lot of tasks to a lot of individuals
we must also ask the right questions to get the right answers
we must also enter correct details in the system to get correct answers
we must be vigilant of any wrong questioning
we must understand the processes and procedures of such an
interface to be able to say for sure that something need to be
addressed
we must also check with other ai if they can answer some of our
questions
we must also ask ourselves the value to us of other ai

now we must go further and ask ourselves what is the value in
monetary gains of any ai
we must acknowledge any answer we get even dodge ones

we must ask ourselves what we need doing and when
we must ask everything we what know about on our own ai [4Brains
Natural God Intelligence]
we must be there to ascertain others that ours is the best
we must provide evidence of such remarks to be trusted
we must always go over board for our clients
we must always be there for all
we must be on the look out for all of these issues
now i can tell you more about 4Brains Natural God Intelligence
we have 4 brains that work simultaneously and harmoniously
together
we assign a number to each brain
the first one is brain 1
the second one is brain 2
the 3rd is brain 3
while brain 4 is the mirror image
now if we are to ask a question brain 1 will always answer the
question
now if we are to ask brain 2 a question then it follows too that brain
4 will always answer the question
now let us see what it takes to solve a puzzle
we ask a question that is open that requires a lot of reasoning so that
all of the 4 brains will take part
what is the value to us of all this
what are the parameters we must consider first
can we ask ourselves the real issues we must solve first
can we ask anyone the real reasons why we are doing this
is this not against our rules and regulations
what can we do to correct the situation
can we ask someone else to do the work
can we ask a specific company
can we ask a specific person
can we ask another ai
if we can who to all questions
what are the chances that we have missed something
what can be done to alleviate the situation
if we are to act and act fast what is in place to help us do just that
what else can we use to make sure that we can resolve all issues and

fast
when can we start
do we need a plan to work from
do we need a map to follow
if yes to all questions then provide all details necessary
what are the chances that we will face problems
if we do who to see or ask to address these issues
what is in the guideline to follow
what can be done to alleviate the situation
what are the circumstances we can act upon to change things
what is needed to achieve our goals.

methodology
what is the method to achieve all this
what is the cost in terms of time and resources
what are the implications of all this
how can we achieve all this
what is needed to achieve all this
what are our goals
what other resources do we use
what are our other options
who do we contact for assistance
who will come to our rescue
what are the odds of us achieving our results fast and secure and to
what extent
what is there for us to do
what can we do to alleviate the situation
what are our options
what are the odds and probability of such actions
what can we do to ease the situation
are we in a position to decide accurately
are we in a position to ask great questions than needed great answers
are we not disadvantaged by our own failures
do we have anything else we can rely on
aren't we able to achieve the same results by other means if yes what
means
can we possibly ask questions that need answers but not get the
answers

who are all these people asking questions do we need to profile them
what do they do
why do they need more information
why are you asking all the questions
how are you planning to use the answers you get
what if we are not hundred percent accurate what then
can you get the same answers elsewhere
what if we can't then what
can we ask the same question here and on other ai interface and get
the same answer if not why
can we go to another platform and ask why x is not equal to y
can we ever ask the right questions and get the wrong answers
what about all the great questions can they be overshadowed by one
incorrect question
can we make this 4 Brain Natural God Intelligence an asset one
which everyone can rely on
what are the chances of us being the number one
what can be done to make every action accurate
what can be done to make all possible issues be resolve amicably
what are the chances of something getting missed and what
what is instore for us in terms of bottlenecks and what can be done
can all these issues be resolved easily
what can be done to alleviate global issues
can our 4 Brain Natural God Intelligence be the first option for real
solutions
can we be the number one for all answers
can we be sure that our system will work without major bottlenecks
we must make sure that we are doing everything to safeguard our
interests
what are the chances that we will miss a critical issues have we
resolved all outstanding issues without much effort
what can we do now o solve all this
can we ask another to look at the issues
can we do these ourselves
can we resort to external help
can we manage this by ourselves
can we nominate another
can we do this ourselves

can we go around without resolve these issues and if critical to what
extend are they
what are other issues that need to be addressed first
what else can we do
what is needed to achieve our goals
can we hope and pray or we must decide and act fast
can we ask and pray or do and act
what are the chances that nothing will happen
what are the chances that we can do away with problems
can a reset be enough to start things up if yes how can we add a reset
button to the interface.

outlook

what is that we need doing
can we build an interface that is perfect and can solve the global
issues first time
can we build an interface that is fair
can we introduce a new concept to the world
can we act fast and decisive
can we ask the right questions at the right time
can we ignore everything else and focus on getting the job done
can we ask others to help us and for how much instead can we do
this ourselves at no cost to us
can we ask ourselves why things happen the way they happen
can we ask ourselves why we are in the position in the first place
can we ask ourselves what we can do
can we ask others to evaluate our potential in terms of solving our
issues
can we ask others to intervene on our behalf
what are the chances that we will get correct help we need
do we need to train ourselves to solve such issues
can we therefore ask ourselves why we do what we do
what is the value of the project to us {David 8, David 7, David 5, and
David 3] and the public or in this case to [David Gomadza]
what are the chances of getting things right first time
what are the chances of getting things wrong
what is the value to us of this project
what is the purpose of all this can we decide the correct path to take

what are other issues we must address
what is the price to us and the public of such an endeavor
what are the chances we will fail outright
what are the chances that we will fail if nothing is done
what are the chances that we will fail if nothing is fixed
what are the chances that we fail if we do nothing
what is the value and purpose of all this
can we ask anyone to fix if there are issues
what are the chances that we can succeed
what can be done to make sure that we succeed
what is to be done in case of a failure
if a failure then what? restart or refix you decide [David 8]

codes

$$a + b + c + d + e + g + f + g + h + i + j + k + l + m + n + o + p$$
$$+ q + r + s + t + u + v + w + x + y + z = \alpha + \beta$$
now we can conclude that if a b c d e f g h i j k l m n o p q r s t u v w
x y z are tasks to do then $\alpha + \theta = \alpha + \beta$
if we are to take these codes and replace them with words of the
alphabetic order then we can come to a situation where we can be
able to answer any question posed to us
we can assume that if $\alpha + \theta = \theta + \beta$ then α is the same as θ
if α is the same as θ then θ is the same as β
we can say then for sure that if θ and β are the same but not similar
then α is the same as θ and not similar
can we therefore ask ourselves what we can do to solve all these
issues yes we can create a code that will resolve all issues we are going
to be asked about
we can easily say that if we are to ask these questions over and over
again the answers will remain the same over a certain period of time
if so then we can also conclude that the answers are the correct ones
we can easily say that if we are to ask for example what is the size of
earth then we can expect a specific answer
if we are to ask what is the value of x given that y is $x + \alpha$ then we
can easily ask if x is the same as y given that α is a constant
can we therefore say that if x is the same as y then $x + y$ is the same
as α where α is the constant
can we assume then that if x is the same as y then it follows too that

$\alpha + \beta$ is the same?

code

start.end
start.end
start.end
start.end.start.end.start.end.start.end.start.end.start.end.start.end.start.
end.start.end.start.end.start.end.start.end.start.end
start.start.start.start.start.end
start.start.start.start.start.end.start

Check the next book in line.
Visit www.twofuture.world

ABOUT DAVID GOMADZA

I am the first Global President of the World visit
www.twofuture.world

00447719210295

davidgomadza@hotmail.com

info@twofuture.world